Queen Esther
saves her people

Story by Penny Frank

Illustrated by Tony Morris

THE LION
STORY BIBLE

28

TRING · BELLEVILLE · SYDNEY

The Bible tells us how God chose the Jewish nation to be his special people. He made them a promise that he would always love and care for them. But they must obey him.

Esther was a Jewish girl who became queen in the far-off land of Persia. You can find the story in your own Bible in the book called by her name.

Copyright © 1986 Lion Publishing

Published by
Lion Publishing plc
Icknield Way, Tring, Herts, England
ISBN 0 85648 753 8
Lion Publishing Corporation
10885 Textile Road, Belleville,
Michigan 48111, USA
ISBN 0 85648 753 8
Albatross Books
PO Box 320, Sutherland, NSW 2232, Australia
ISBN 0 86760 537 5

First edition 1986

Printed and bound in Hong Kong
by Mandarin Offset International (HK) Ltd

**British Library Cataloguing in
Publication Data**

Frank, Penny
　Queen Esther saves her people. –
　(The Lion Story Bible; 28)
　1. Esther – Juvenile literature
　2. Bible stories, English – O.T. Esther
　I. Title　　II. Morris, Tony
　222'.90924　　BS580.E8

ISBN 0-85648-753-8

Library of Congress Cataloging in
Publication Data

Frank, Penny.
Queen Esther saves her people.
(The Lion Story Bible; 28)
1. Esther, Queen of Persia – Juvenile
literature.
2. Bible. O.T. – Biography – Juvenile
literature.
3. Bible stories, English – O.T. Esther.
[1. Esther, Queen of Persia. 2. Bible
stories – O.T.] I. Morris, Tony, ill.
II. Title. III. Series: Frank, Penny.
Lion Story Bible; 28.
BS580.E8F73 1986 222'.909505
85-13153
ISBN 0-85648-753-8

One day, in the city of Susa, there was great excitement. The king of Persia was going to choose a new queen.

The most beautiful girls in the land were sent to the palace. For a whole year they were given special food. They were made even more beautiful, ready for King Xerxes to choose the one he liked best.

One of the girls sent to the palace was called Esther. She was Jewish. Her parents had died when she was a little girl, so she lived with her uncle.

'You are so beautiful, I'm sure the king will choose you,' said her uncle, Mordecai. 'But don't tell him you are Jewish. Keep that a secret.'

Esther did as Mordecai told her. She
kept her secret. King Xerxes chose her
out of all the other girls, because she
was so lovely.

The whole city had a holiday. The
king gave everyone presents to celebrate
his new queen, Esther.

Esther enjoyed living at the palace. Her uncle, Mordecai, worked there. He told Esther what was happening in other parts of the busy palace.

One day he was very worried.

'I have just heard two men planning to kill the king,' he said.

6

Immediately Esther told the king. When he found out that the story was true, he punished the two men.

The king told his servant to write down Mordecai's name in his diary, so that he would not forget the man who had saved his life.

A few years later, King Xerxes had a new Prime Minister. His name was Haman, and he was proud and wicked.

When Haman walked in the palace gardens and in the city square, he made everyone bow down to him.

But Mordecai did not bow down to
Haman.

'I bow down only to the living God,'
he told the people. 'I cannot bow down
to Haman.' So Haman hated him.

Haman decided it was time to get rid of
Mordecai and all his people. He went to
the king.

'Scattered across your land,' he told
the king, 'are people who do not live like
us. They do not obey the laws of the
land, and as I am your Prime Minister
I advise you to get rid of them.'

Haman was a clever man. When he spoke like that, King Xerxes thought the idea was very sensible. He gave the order that on a certain day all the Jews should be killed.

When Mordecai heard of the king's order, he was very upset. Mordecai went to see Esther.

'This is all Haman's fault,' said Mordecai. 'He wouldn't dare to do it if he knew that you were a Jewish girl, too. You must go and ask the king to save our lives.'

'I am only allowed to go to the king if he asks for me,' said Queen Esther. 'He may kill me if I go without an invitation. You must ask all our people to pray for me.'

'Of course we will pray for you,' said Mordecai. 'Perhaps this is why God made you queen of Persia: so that you could save our people.'

Esther went quietly to the king's room. She knew she was breaking the palace rules. She was so thankful when he looked pleased to see her.

'What would you like, Esther?' said the king.

'Please come to a special banquet I am having,' said Queen Esther. 'I would like you to bring Haman with you.'

The king and Haman came to the
banquet. It was a delicious meal. Haman
felt very proud of being at the queen's
banquet.

That night King Xerxes could not get to
sleep. He tossed and turned, grunted and
yawned, but still he was wide awake. In
the end he started to read his diary.

He read about the two men who had
plotted to kill him.

'Have I ever rewarded Mordecai?' he
asked his servant.

'No, never,' the servant said.

The next day King Xerxes gave
Mordecai some gorgeous robes and put
him on his own horse. He told Haman to
go ahead of the horse around the city
square, shouting, 'Look how the king
rewards a man who serves him well.'
Haman just hated doing that.

The next night the king and Haman went to see the queen again.

'I want to give you a present,' the king said to Esther. 'You can have anything you like. What can I give you?'

Esther was trembling with fear. She knew she must tell the king now about the plot to kill the Jews.

'There is only one present I really want,'
Esther said. 'I am a Jew. I want you to
change the order which says all the Jews
must be killed.'

'Who told me to make such a terrible
order?' asked the king.

'That man did,' said Queen Esther,
and pointed at Haman.

The king looked at Haman. Haman was trying to run away. The servants in the palace caught him.

'He wanted to kill my queen and Mordecai and all the Jews!' shouted the king. 'Get rid of him instead.'

So Mordecai was made Prime Minister in place of Haman.

The advice he gave the king was always wise and good. God's people were safe, living in the land of Persia.

Esther was given all the riches which
had belonged to Haman.

She was so glad she had trusted the
living God to keep her safe when she
was frightened. And she thanked God
every day, because he had saved his
people.

The Lion Story Bible is made up of 52 individual stories for young readers, building up an understanding of the Bible as one story — God's story — a story for all time and all people.

The Old Testament section (numbers 1–30) tells the story of a great nation — God's chosen people, the Israelites — and God's love and care for them through good times and bad. The stories are about people who knew and trusted God. From this nation came one special person, Jesus Christ, sent by God to save all people everywhere.

The story of Queen Esther comes from the Old Testament book of Esther. God's people the Jews (they were given that name because they came from the kingdom of Judah) were in exile, under the rule of the king of Persia. But although they were far from home, God had not forgotten about them. He was still looking after them.

This time, though, he went about it in an unusual way — through a pretty girl who won a beauty contest. God was making sure that when the vital moment came, and their enemies were all set to wipe out his people, someone was there to speak to the king.

The next story in the series, number 29: *Nehemiah's greatest day*, tells the exciting story of how God's people went back to Jerusalem and built their city once again.